Spousal Immigration – Doing It Right

Stephen J. Zawacki, Esq.

And

Linda Yin Liang, Esq.

Copyright

This publication is designed to provide accurate information, not legal advice. For legal advice, be sure to consult with a qualified attorney who is experienced in American immigration law. Also, although all reasonable actions to keep this book as accurate as possible, the reader should be advised that immigration law is very dynamic and changes often.

ISBN-13: 978-1470076160

Dedication

Our thanks to the legal profession, particularly all of the immigration attorneys who over the years shared their knowledge and skills with us.

Preface

This book represents the experience of many years as two American immigration attorneys. We have had the privilege of assisting countless couples to achieve family unity in the United States. Being an immigration attorney is a wonderful way to make a living!

The marriage petitioning process has always been subject to much confusion, rumor, doubt and misconception. Yesterday's rules do not apply today – the rules may change again tomorrow. If this book makes the process more understandable, then it has accomplished its goal.

Many times throughout this book we have stressed the need to contact a qualified immigration attorney at certain points throughout the process. This recommendation is not intended to provide business opportunities for attorneys, but rather to emphasize the seriousness of those points.

Immigration is a legal action and the United States is a land of laws. The counsel of a qualified attorney during a legal action that may affect the lives of many persons is logical and prudent.

TABLE OF CONTENTS

Page

CHAPTER ONE – Introduction to the Process

Do I love him enough to marry him?

Does he love me for <u>me</u> - or because I can get him a green card?

What if she <u>doesn't</u> get her green card?

For U.S. citizens and lawful permanent residents (called "LPRs"), United States law allows them to petition for their husbands and wives to come to the USA and receive lawful permanent residence ("Green Card") status. LPRs are allowed to live indefinitely and work in the USA.

The history of the "Marriage Green Card" has been a stormy one. The fear of introducing any communicable diseases into America, the exploitation of young Americans living temporarily overseas by schemers who only want to get across the border, and ethnic prejudices have all affected U.S. immigration law. The law, known as the Immigration and Naturalization Act (as amended), provides for a supposedly streamlined and orderly process to allow foreign-born spouses of Americans and Lawful Permanent Residents (LPRs) admittance as immigrants into the United States. However, the "green card" process is far from being streamlined, and is often compared to a dirt road, full of potential potholes and detours.

Both U.S. citizens and lawful permanent residents (LPRs) can sponsor their spouses for immigration visas. However, there is a major difference - spouses of U.S. citizens can get an immediate visa and entry into the USA, while spouses of LPRs are placed on a "waiting list" that can take many years before a visa is available for them.

This book acts as a narrative map down the "marriage green card" road. Accompanying us will be our guides - two typical private persons who will travel down the marriage road and the U.S. Government officials who will be the "traffic police" they will encounter.

Our marriage-minded persons are Miss Freda Foreigner and Mister Chester Citizen.

Miss Freda Foreigner can be described as a woman in love with a U.S. citizen. She plans to marry her American boyfriend and move to the United States as his spouse. Miss Foreigner has never been a resident of the United States and this is her first experience with the American immigration system.

Mister Chester Citizen is typical of an American citizen in love with a woman who is not an American citizen and resides in another country. He plans to marry his foreign girlfriend. This is also Mister Citizen's first experience with the American immigration system.

((Note; While our players are shown as American and LPR males and a non-American female, the roles could just as easily been reversed. The examples within this book were chosen as those most commonly encountered.))

As with most bureaucracies, there are many activities that can be effectively accomplished by one government agency, but oftentimes more than one agency finds itself with some but-not-all of the responsibilities. These responsibilities may overlap, and there can be rivalries between the agencies as to whose rules apply in a given situation. Immigration is one of those lucky activities.

The Department of Homeland Security's Citizenship and Immigration Service (USCIS) handles all immigration processing originating in the United States.

The Department of State's Consular Affairs Branch has the honor of performing immigration processing at all U.S. embassies and consulates worldwide.

Agent America shall be our generic government official. He (or she, depending on the locale) would have the title of "USCIS Inspector/Examiner" in the United States, or "Consular Officer" at a U.S. embassy or consulate. It is his/her job to conduct interviews, process the paperwork and make judgment calls on the truth or falsity of statements or evidence given to him/her by our lovebirds.

How the immigration process works is described in the remaining chapters:

Chapter Two describes what is a marriage in the eyes of the American immigration system.

Chapters Three through Six cover specific time frames in the immigration-processing of a marriage-based visa: Courtship and Marriage, Forms Preparation, The Marriage Interview and Denial.

Chapter Seven provides some typical "questions and answers" to marriage-related immigration topics.

So, onward we go.....

CHAPTER TWO – An American Marriage, Immigration Style

The Law

American law allows US citizens to sponsor their spouses for an immediate visa and entry into the United States.

American Law also allows lawful permanent residents (LPRs) to sponsor their spouses, but these spouses must wait until a visa is available before they can enter the United States. This wait can be many years.

All marriage-based immigrant petitions center on whether the marriage is a legitimate one, or one entered solely so that Miss Foreigner can get a green card.

The Government's Decision

Agent America has a crucial decision to make. Is Miss Foreigner's and Mister Citizen's relationship "real," in the sense that the two spouses have known each other long enough and have shared enough experiences to truly be in love and committed to marriage? Is their relationship a "sham," in the sense that the lovebirds are simply trying to fool Agent America in granting Miss Foreigner entry into the United States? If Agent America's decision is that the marriage is a "real" marriage, then the processing of Miss Foreigner's immigrant visa will occur without delay.

If Agent America believes that a "sham marriage" exists, or that there is a strong potential that a "sham marriage" may exist, then our lovebirds have a serious problem. First of all, at minimum the processing will take longer, and also become much more expensive to our lovebirds.

Second, and more importantly, Miss Foreigner may be permanently banned from ever getting a green card, and Mister Citizen may be prosecuted for committing fraud upon the American Government!

The facts and information available to Agent America, both in the documents provided during the petitioning process and the testimony given during interviews, shall determine what this decision will be.

Real or Sham Marriage

A newspaper ad looking for a spouse, and willing to pay $5,000.00 for a "quickie marriage..."

One friend "helping" another by a "marriage in name only..."

An "arranged marriage" where the spouses don't live together...

Sham relationship scams have been popular for many years, and the Agent Americas of the world have a lot of experience in recognizing these scams. Miss Foreigner and Mister Citizen may think they can convince Agent America in believing a relationship exists where there is none. This would be foolhardy!

Agent America has the benefit of a lot of training in how to recognize sham marriage scams, and probably has years of experience in evaluating other marriage-based petitions. While our government agent may occasionally be fooled, it is only occasionally. If our lovebirds try and fail to fool Agent America, they must remember that the penalties for immigration marriage fraud can be a fine of up to US$ 250,000.00 and up to five years in jail! Also, Miss Foreigner can be banned from ever coming into the United States for the rest of her life!

The Agent America personnel are immigration professionals, and our lovebirds are immigration amateurs. Who usually wins in any contest between an amateur and a professional? Enough said!

Throughout the immigration process, the lovebirds will have to prove the sincerity and validity of the marriage. It is not the responsibility of Agent America to prove the marriage was created solely to get an immigration benefit. The burden of proof that the marriage is "real" falls on our lovebirds. That means our lovebirds will need evidence to prove their case.

We don't often think of a marriage as needing evidence to prove itself to others, but in the case of gaining a benefit from the American immigration system, this evidence is critical. Agent America probably has never met either of the new spouses before, and the agent's first opinions will be made only on the paperwork provided. Examples of Agent America's initial questions are:

1) How much time has elapsed between when the spouses first met and the date of the marriage?

2) What is the age difference between the spouses?

3) Is this a "cross-cultural" marriage?

4) How much time have the spouses spent much time together before the marriage?

5) Was the marriage "brokered?"

6) How many times has each spouse been married?

7) Has Miss Foreigner ever been previously married to an American?

8) Has Miss Foreigner ever been deported?

Oftentimes, when a person asks a question, a conservative answer with a lot of details is expected. However, what usually happens is that the person answering the question only wants to provide the minimum information possible to the question. This is especially true during immigration processing.

Most likely, Miss Foreigner will become both angry and embarrassed when Agent America asks questions about intimate details of her relationship with her new spouse. Mister Citizen will also be upset that Agent America is peeking too closely into people's private lives.

Both Agent America and our lovebirds are in a no-win situation. Agent America must make a decision based on facts and experience, while our lovebirds don't want their private lives a matter of public record and scrutiny.

In the end, the question is who will lose the most in this battle of wills? For Agent America, it is a "business as usual" situation. Agent America will not lose his job or any money over a bad decision. Agent America only has to answer to his/her supervisor, and the standard practice is to make conservative, non-controversial decisions. Agent America will not stick his/her neck out, no matter how much Mr. Citizen may threaten him or Miss Foreigner may beg.

In some countries the way to change a bureaucrat's mind is to give him/her money. If Miss Foreigner tries to "influence" Agent America in this manner, the result will be catastrophic. Not only will the petition and visa be denied, if the attempted bribery occurs in the United States, Miss Foreigner may get arrested and end up in jail.

Miss Foreigner and Mister Citizen, on the other hand, have a lot at stake. The cost of maintaining separate households, travel plans, and many other factors will be impacted if Agent America is not satisfied with the answers to his/her questions.

There is no mandatory time requirement forcing Agent America to make his/her decision by a given date. Agent America is free to take as much time as s/he believes is necessary to thoroughly examine the facts of each case. Miss Foreigner's processing time can be lengthened by several months (even years!) if Agent America stalls, or worse yet, make a ruling that the marriage is a "sham marriage."

Many people have found that having a consultation with an experienced immigration attorney before submitting any petition for Miss Foreigner is money well spent. Some people, even before the marriage occurs, discuss the situation of both potential spouses with an immigration attorney. The idea is, a little planning in the beginning is better than a lot of reaction later.

A determination of a "sham marriage" should not be taken lightly. The penalties, long and short term, are severe and long-lasting.

CHAPTER THREE – Courtship and Marriage

Marriage is supposed to be a lifetime commitment made between two persons to love, honor and protect the other. In the American Government's viewpoint, a marriage commitment also requires that persons have previously been in a relationship that:

1) developed over a "reasonable" period of time; and

2) involved "reasonable" personal contact between the persons.

The term "reasonable" is a legal word of art, and the interpretation of this word often varies from case to case. Since every culture and ethnic group has a different concept of what a courtship involves, "reasonableness" in relationship development can require a lot of analysis.

In several cultures, a courtship is a very structured activity. It may take many months, sometimes years, to ripen into a relationship leading to marriage.

In other cultures, the amount of contact between the potential marriage-mates is much more spontaneous. The amount of time potential spouses may spend together before marriage may be very brief (compared to other cultures). This is especially true when the marriage may have been arranged through family intermediaries or marriage-brokers.

Agent America must take these differences into account when determining "reasonableness," especially regarding the length of time that Miss Foreigner and Mister Citizen know each other or are together. What Agent America tries to determine is whether the relationship would exist if there was no need or desire for a United States green card.

In other words, would Miss Foreigner and Mister Citizen still get married if Miss Foreigner did not have to become a lawful permanent resident in order to live with her husband?

If the answer is "Yes," then Miss Foreigner is well on her way to receiving a shiny new American immigrant visa in her passport.

If the answer is "No," then Miss Foreigner will not get her immigrant visa. Also, if the Agent America believes that the lovebirds were intentionally trying to break any immigration laws, then Mister Citizen may be prosecuted for attempting to defraud the American Government.

So, the most effective way to prove the legitimacy of a marriage involving an American Citizen and a foreigner is to have evidence proving that a solid relationship existed prior to the marriage. Evidence of a relationship can take many forms. The most common types of evidence are:

- Letters and Correspondence

- Tickets and Receipts

- Photographs

- Affidavits

The evidence does not have to be perfect. There is no need for the proof of the relationship to document every emotional moment of our lovebirds. Indeed, if the proof was that perfect, Agent America may not believe it and may want to research the authenticity of key items. People just don't keep perfect records on their love lives! So, if the proof reads like a romantic bestseller, then it will raise a questioning eyebrow as probably being fabricated especially for Agent America.

Remember, Agent America is human. S/he only wants to feel comfortable in his/her determination as to the "bona fides" of the relationship. S/he doesn't want to know all of the intimate details of our lovebirds' courtship. As long as there are no glaring deficiencies in our lovebirds' evidence, and there aren't obvious contradictions, our lovebirds will receive the paternal blessing of Uncle Sam!

Letters and Correspondence

The romantic in Agent America believes that people in love write love letters to each other. The existence of letters written by Miss Foreigner and Mister Citizen during their relationship, or a relationship in the making, provides proof that they have known each other during the letter-writing period.

In today's Internet-driven world, e-mail has replaced handwritten correspondence for many people. Copies of e-mails can also be given to Agent America if e-mail between the lovebirds have been exchanged.

Now, Agent America is not naive. S/he will check letters to see if the dates correspond to any information provided on Miss Foreigner's visa petition. S/he will also ask questions about the contents of these letters during Miss Foreigner's marriage interview. S/he will check postmarks on envelopes. S/he will check to see any other obvious errors such as letters written by both persons using the same paper, ink or typewriter. S/he will check e-mail routing symbols to see if they are accurate. As silly as it may seem, people have shown Agent America different letters supposedly written by each of the lovebirds, however all the letters written are in one person's handwriting!

If the letters available were written solely by Miss Foreigner (or Mister Citizen), then the odds that the letters will be believed by Agent America as legitimate are not good. Letters from both persons provide much greater credibility of the existence of a relationship. If available, the envelopes, since they have dated postmarks and return addresses, provide substantial evidence of the legitimacy of the letters.

So, Miss Foreigner and Mister Citizen need to keep all their letters and cards. Chances are, these letters may have more than personal value. They may become the proof that satisfies Agent America that our lovebirds' relationship is reasonable to result in marriage.

Tickets and Receipts

Letters between persons are nice, but if Miss Foreigner and Mister Citizen have proof that they have been together anywhere at any time, that's even better.

16

Agent America has a difficult time believing that people who never have been physically in the presence of each other can develop a relationship strong enough to declare undying love and desire to marry. One of the checklist items for Agent America is to verify that the lovebirds have indeed been together at least once prior to the decision to marry.

Let's suppose that Miss Foreigner and Mister Citizen first met in Paris. They met again at a later date, during a rock concert in London. They also vacationed together in Cancun and Tahiti. As a result of all of these travels and joint adventures, they should have receipts, ticket stubs, hotel bills, airline boarding passes, passport stamps and all sorts of evidence that each of them were in the same place at the same time.

The fact that Miss Foreigner and Mister Citizen can prove that each of them were physically in the same locations at the same time makes their claim of relationship more plausible. In fact, without such proof, Agent America may not approve Mister Citizen's petition for Miss Foreigner's visa to come to the United States. Also, Agent America will specifically ask Miss Foreigner to prove that she has met and been with Mister Citizen prior to the visa application.

Tickets and receipts may not have been saved during the relationship. However, with a little work they can be recovered. As examples:

- Anything paid by credit card can be verified through credit card bill summaries.

- Airline tickets acquired through a travel agency can be proven by the travel agency's records.

- Company vacation records showing that both persons were not at work when they claimed to be vacationing together can be linked as proof.

- Canceled checks for payment of expenses or activities may provide corroboration of these activities, especially if the "memo" section of the check has a reference of the other person.

- Passports are stamped upon arrival into a country, and can prove being in-country at a certain time frame.

So, never underestimate the value of good record-keeping!

Photographs

Someone once said that words are nice, but pictures can be worth thousands of words. Photographs of Miss Foreigner and Mister Citizen together, sharing activities, provide strong evidence that our lovebirds have a relationship "reasonably" leading to marriage. The classic tourist snapshots are the best, such as our lovebirds hugging each other atop the Eiffel Tower, or sharing a ski-lift seat at Vail, or holding hands while standing in front of Saint Basil's Cathedral.

If Miss Foreigner has any pictures or snapshots that show Mister Citizen and her together, she should be sure to have them ready to bring to her immigration interview. Agent America will examine the photos for any doctoring or editing, and also for any date stamps that are often placed on photos by the film processors.

Miss Foreigner should double-check any dates on photos (front and back) to be sure the dates verify her claims of togetherness. Also, she should check that any dates stated in affidavits match with the dates on the photographs.

Affidavits

An affidavit is a statement given by a person to verify a fact or knowledge of event. This statement is signed in the presence of a Notary Public or other official with similar authority who verifies the signature and identity of the person making the statement.

Affidavits are valuable when they confirm information provided within the visa petition for Miss Foreigner. If a witness can confirm that on a specific day s/he saw Miss Foreigner and Mister Citizen together on the Eiffel Tower, behaving like close friends, then his/her testimony can be used to supplement the claims of our lovebirds.

The format and content of an affidavit are important. An affidavit needs to clearly identify the person making the statement. The statement itself needs to be prepared in a clear and concise manner, allowing for only one interpretation of the facts. Also, the acknowledgment of the notary must be according to the legal requirements where the affidavit is prepared and signed. If there are any doubts on how to prepare an affidavit, check with a lawyer.

The Marriage

It may seem silly to think that Mister Citizen may petition for Miss Foreigner's visa when he's not legally married to her. However, this situation happens every day.

Agent America will examine Mister Citizen's petition to verify that our lovebirds' marriage met the legal requirements where the marriage occurred. Also, Miss Foreigner and Mister citizen will have to prove that any prior marriages were legally terminated before they married.

The issue of prior marriages causes more immigration sponsorship problems than anything else. The laws of divorce, dissolution of marriage, and annulment vary dramatically around the world, and even from state-to-state within the United States.

A divorce that is valid in one place may not be valid in another. As an example, let's say that Miss Foreigner has always been single, but Mister Citizen was married to his first wife according to the laws of California. The first wife had left Mister Citizen and got a divorce in the Dominican Republic by proxy representation. Mister Citizen and Miss Foreigner then get married in Ecuador.

According to American immigration law, Miss Foreigner and Mister Citizen can only be married to one person at a time. For the example, Agent America will question whether Mister Citizen is still legally married to his first wife, since a by-proxy divorce may not be valid in the United States, leaving the original California marriage as still in effect.

The next question is whether Ecuador recognizes Mr. Citizen's divorce as valid. If Agent America has any doubts, then expect him/her to say that: 1) Mr. Citizen's first marriage is still valid; 2) the Citizen/Foreigner marriage is bigamy; and 3) Miss Foreigner cannot have a marriage-based immigrant visa.

The result is now confusion for Miss Foreigner and Mister Citizen, combined with considerable delay and expense in eventually getting Miss Foreigner her immigrant visa.

There is also the potential of Miss Foreigner never getting her immigrant visa due to all of Mister Citizen's not-quite-a-divorce problems.

Marriage Brokers

Many cultures use intermediaries to recruit, interview and select potential mates for family members. The hopeful image of such a mate-search is that of a cautious family whose goal is to protect the future husband or wife from a scurrilous or "unworthy" person. In other words, it's "gold-digger" prevention in a most thorough manner.

Agent America will try to determine whether the use of an intermediary was part of an accepted cultural practice, or part of a green card acquisition scheme.

Mister Citizen may be attempting to acquire a bride by answering a magazine advertisement for "Beautiful Asian Girls Want To Marry Americans - Call 1-800-555-5555."

Miss Foreigner may be husband-hunting through a newspaper ad stating, "Do You Want A Green Card? American Men Want You! Reply to Box 1234 at This Newspaper."

If a commercial marriage broker was hired by Mister Citizen to find him a foreign bride, then Agent America will look very carefully at the petition. Marriages for profit are not considered as valid marriages for immigration purposes. When the marriage happens (or will happen) after either person responds to a marriage agency's advertisement, the chances of Agent America recognizing the marriage as legitimate are very slim.

There is another, more grisly, problem that may arise from a brokered marriage - spouse abuse. When two people who don't know each other get married and start living together, neither one has any idea of how their new spouse will behave. The kind words in a written proposal and gentle behavior at the marriage ceremony may hide a fiend. Miss Foreigner (now Mrs. Citizen) may find herself married to a monster who gets his thrills from wife-beating or worse.

So, although having to show proof of a true relationship may seem old-fashioned, the logic of doing so is contained in many volumes of criminal court and hospital records.

Summary

American immigration law has taken the romance out of courtship and marriage, and has reformatted it into a "system" similar to a computer program. Understanding this "system" may not be possible, but recognizing its existence makes it much easier for Miss Foreigner to succeed in getting her immigrant visa.

If either Miss Foreigner or Mister Citizen is unsure whether the courtship or marriage is sufficient (legally) to get Miss Foreigner her immigrant visa, then a consultation with a qualified immigration attorney would be worthwhile.

CHAPTER FOUR – Forms Preparation

Processing Miss Foreigner's immigrant visa requires the preparation of several government forms. Each form has to be completed at different times during the processing.

The United States Government occasionally changes its forms requirements, and oftentimes the forms themselves. Also, each embassy and consulate may have special requirements that are unique to the country where located. Miss Foreigner should contact the embassy or consulate located within her home country to learn what, if any, special processing is needed at that location.

The United States Citizenship and Immigration Service provides all of the necessary forms for free download at it's Internet website – http://www.uscis.gov – as well as current information regarding immigration to the USA. USCIS does not provide legal information or services, but the information at its website can answer many common questions.

The following provides a summary about certain forms that are common to all marriage-based immigrant visa petitions. It is important to remember that many of these forms have separate fees that must be paid before the form will be processed.

Petition for Alien Relative

A Petition for Alien Relative acts as the foundation for all subsequent actions.

Currently, the form for this action is Form I-130. It is prepared and submitted by Mister Citizen to the United States Citizenship and Immigration Service (USCIS).

This form asks information concerning Mister Citizen and Miss Foreigner. It asks for proof of how Mister Citizen claims citizenship (birth or naturalization).

This form also asks for detailed information concerning the marriage of Miss Foreigner and Mister Citizen. Several documents must be provided with the Form I-130 including (but not limited to): 1) special USCIS passport-style photographs of both Miss Foreigner and Mister Citizen; 3) a certified copy of the marriage license; 4) copies of any divorce decrees; 5) and copies of both spouse's birth certificates.

All documents that are not in English must include a certified English translation with the foreign-language document.

Affidavit of Support

As unromantic as it may be, Mr. Citizen must prove that he can support a wife, or Miss Foreigner will never get a green card. American law requires Mr. Citizen to show that he makes enough money to afford a wife (and any stepchildren) before a green card will be issued to Miss Foreigner.

The affidavit of support is a very serious document. It is actually a contract between Mr. Citizen and the American Government. This contract states that no public money (welfare, medicaid, etc.) can be spent on Miss Foreigner while the contract is in effect. If any public money is spent on Miss Foreigner, the American Government can collect what was spent from Mr. Citizen.

The affidavit of support stays in effect until one of four things happens: 1) Miss Foreigner becomes an American citizen; 2) Miss Foreigner works for approximately ten years and contributes into the Social Security fund during that time; 3) Miss Foreigner's loses her lawful permanent resident status (e.g., is deported or abandons her U.S. residence, etc.); or 4) Miss Foreigner dies.

If Mr. Citizen and Miss Foreigner get divorced after she gets her green card, the affidavit of support still remains valid!

The amount of money Mr. Citizen must make to sponsor his wife changes each year. Every April, the American Government publishes a report with that year's income requirements. This report is available at every American embassy/consulate, every USCIS office and the USCIS Internet website (http://www.uscis.gov).

If Mr. Citizen does not make enough money according to the government rules, then he must either: 1) find another American citizen or lawful permanent resident who is willing to submit a supplemental affidavit of support; or 2) explain to Miss Foreigner that she cannot get her green card because he is too poor to sponsor her.

Visa Application

Normally, the processing of a marriage-based immigrant visa finds Miss Foreigner outside of the United States. Miss Foreigner then must receive her visa at the embassy or consulate nearest her home. This is referred to as "consular processing" and must follow the rules established at the servicing American embassy/consulate. Consular processing instructions are available at the embassy/consulate's information window or Internet website.

Adjustment of Status

There are instances when Miss Foreigner is residing in the United States (legally or illegally) when she marries Mister Citizen. When that happens, Miss Foreigner may be eligible to complete her immigrant visa processing in the United States at a USCIS office, rather than return to her home country. This is called "adjustment of status."

At present, adjustment of status is only available (with a couple of exceptions) for non-citizens who entered the United States legally. By "entering legally," it is meant that the non-citizen arrived at an official United States port-of-entry, was inspected by a U.S. Customs and Border Security inspector, and the inspector allowed the non-citizen to enter the United States.

There used to be a procedure where non-citizens who entered the United States illegally were allowed to seek adjustment of status. That authority ended on January 14, 1998. There are movements within the United States to have this authority reinstated. If Miss Foreigner entered the United States illegally, she should seek the counsel of a qualified immigration attorney before attempting adjustment of status or returning to her home country for consular processing.

Miss Foreigner and Mister Citizen must decide which alternative is financially and personally better for their situation - consular processing or adjustment of status. There are advantages and disadvantages both ways. Consultation with a qualified immigration attorney is recommended before any final decision is made.

Medical Examination

Miss Foreigner, as a routine part of her processing, will be required to have a medical examination by a physician (called a "civil surgeon" by the government) approved by the local American embassy/consulate or by the United States Citizenship and Immigration Service, depending on whether consular processing or adjustment of status applies. Not all physicians are authorized to conduct this examination, so it is important to verify with the embassy/consulate or USCIS that the physician is on the "approved" civil surgeon list. This information is usually available at the embassy/consulate or USCIS Internet website. Miss Foreigner will have to pay for this medical examination.

Part of Miss Foreigner's medical examination is to prove of what inoculations she has had. The United States Center for Disease Control has issued a list of which inoculations are required, depending on which country Miss Foreigner calls home. Inoculations must be current before an immigrant visa can be approved. This list is available at the embassy/consulate's information window or Internet website, as well as at any USCIS office.

When the physician completes the medical examination, this form will be given to Miss Foreigner in a sealed envelope. If the seal is broken or tampered in any way, Agent America will reject the form and its contents. If this happens, a new physical may be required.

If Agent America believed the medical examination report has been altered in any way, s/he may contact the examining physician directly to obtain another copy of this report. If the medical examination report was altered, Agent America may charge Miss Foreigner with fraud and then deny her from receiving an immigrant visa based on the fraud.

Appearance as Representative

If either Miss Foreigner or Mister Citizen wants to have an attorney act as her/his representative during any part of the immigrant visa process, then a form stating so must be submitted. Currently, Form G-28 identifies the case under process, the person being represented, the relationship of the person to the case (petitioner or beneficiary), the name of the attorney, the legal authority for the person to be the attorney, and the extent of representation to be provided.

Unless this form is submitted, the American Government will not discuss any part of Miss Foreigner's or Mister Citizen's case with the attorney. Also, the American Government will not accept any documents from the attorney unless the form has been submitted.

Summary

The paperwork necessary for Miss Foreigner to receive an immigrant visa is immense. Also, the processing of this paperwork is very time-consuming. In other words, nothing happens very quickly and everything is subject to intense scrutiny.

Agent America often receives forms that are incomplete, and may refuse to accept an incomplete form (and any attachments or evidence). An incomplete form can result in long delays. While American law allows private citizens to handle their own paperwork, it may be more timely and cost-efficient to use the services of a qualified immigration attorney instead.

CHAPTER FIVE – The Marriage Interview

When people are romantically involved, they do not often consider that proof of the time they spend together will be needed in the future. These are times of happiness and joy, and not many of us would expect that our courtship experiences may be scrutinized by an unknown bureaucrat. Just the thought of exposing a couple's intimacies to a government official may be enough to sour a relationship.

Once Miss Foreigner and Mister Citizen have started the paperwork to get Miss Foreigner her green card, the lovebirds may get a notice from the American Government to attend an interview regarding the petition.

This government interview is in actuality a marriage fraud interview. Its purpose is to verify that the marriage is legitimate under American immigration law. The interview can be conducted in many ways. Agent America has the option to talk to Miss Foreigner and Mister Citizen together or separate, and to video-record the lovebirds as they respond to questions.

The marriage fraud interview can be highly stressful, even when the marriage is 100% legitimate. Very few people like talking about their private lives to strangers, especially strangers who have power over their future.

Agent America may ask the lovebirds all of the questions contained in the forms previously submitted. In addition, s/he may ask questions regarding any of the courtship and marriage evidence, such as:

- Who took these pictures?

- Why did you take this trip?

- Did you share the hotel room or did you have separate rooms?

- Which airline did you fly?

In other words, the questions will be related to the evidence, but only people who actually shared the experience would know the answers.

Questions have been known to involve intimate details of a relationship, such as:

- On which side of the bed do you sleep?

- What did you have for dinner last night?

- Does she have any tattoos?

- Does he snore?

- Which of her relatives does she dislike the most?

- What was the last gift your wife bought you, and when?

- What his you mother-in-law's first name?

- What is your husband's favorite television show?

Again, the answers to questions such as these require a lot of intimate knowledge about the other person. So, if Miss Foreigner and Mister Citizen do not live together as husband and wife, the chances of them answering questions like these correctly are not good.

It is the responsibility of Miss Foreigner and Mister Citizen to provide the evidence and testimony to convince Agent America that a true relationship was present at the onset of the marriage. It is NOT Agent America's responsibility to prove this relationship does not exist.

Miss Foreigner and Mister Citizen need to present evidence that, when combined with their sworn statements, substantially proves the duration and intensity of their relationship.

In the United States people who live together as husband-and-wife are expected to have paperwork that proves they share a household. If this paperwork does not exist, then Agent America will probably question whether the lovebirds are really married. Examples of such evidence are:

- Photographs (showing both together after marriage)

- apartment lease (signed by both)

- bank statements (joint bank account)

- canceled checks (some checks signed by each person)

- driver's licenses (showing the same address for both)

- insurance papers (showing both names)

The Agent America personnel who conduct these interviews and review visa applications know all the tricks. They have heard many stories and reviewed all types of evidence. It is highly doubtful that Miss Foreigner or Mister Citizen can create phony evidence that won't be revealed as being phony. Not only would that kill Miss Foreigner's chances of receiving a visa, but both of our lovebirds can face criminal charges for attempted fraud upon the American Government.

Agent America can, if s/he desires, have an interview video-recorded. In many USCIS offices there is a standing policy to video-record all adjustment of status interviews. Video-recording provides a means to preserve evidence, and the testimony of Miss Foreigner and Mister Citizen during an interview is evidence that can be used to support a denial of the petition. Also, the video-recording may be used against Miss Foreigner in removal proceedings at Immigration Court.

Miss Foreigner and Mister Citizen must prepare themselves for this interview in the same manner as they would for a job interview. The lovebirds should review all of the documentation they have sent to Agent America. They need to feel comfortable in answering questions verbally that they answered in writing on the various forms. Also, if any additional courtship and marriage evidence is being brought to the interview, the lovebirds need to review the evidence in great detail. Both spouses must be prepared and ready to answer any "when, where, who and why" questions raised by Agent America.

Summary

The marriage interview is like a theater production.   It happens best when the players are well prepared and feel comfortable with the role.

Always remember that Agent America does not know Miss Foreigner or Mister Citizen from Adam and Eve.   This is Agent America's first time in meeting the lovebirds. His/her only knowledge of the lovebirds comes from reading the petition and other forms that have been submitted.

Miss Foreigner and Mister America can make the interview experience much less painful through a lot of preparation. If they have any doubts or fears, the help of an experienced immigration attorney may make the ordeal less traumatic.

CHAPTER SIX - Denial

If there is ever a time when fear and dismay enter a heart, it is when Mister Citizen receives a letter from the United States Citizenship and Immigration Service entitled, "Notice of Intent to Deny."

There is no form number for this document. It normally comes in the format of a letter with "Notice of Intent to Deny" printed as the subject. The purpose of the Notice is to tell the petitioner (in this case, Mister Citizen) that Agent America intends to deny the petition for Miss Foreigner's immigrant visa.

The word "intends" is very important. Agent America has not yet denied the petition. What is being said is that there are problems with the petition, any evidence provided, or testimony given at the marriage fraud interview. These problems are serious enough to create sufficient doubt as to the legitimacy of the marriage, or some other fact which may bar the issuance of Miss Foreigner's immigrant visa.

Agent America is now giving Mister Citizen an opportunity to answer any allegations raised in the Notice. Mister Citizen will be told of these problems in detail within this Notice and given a summary of the applicable law regarding the item(s) of concern.

The Notice will also state that Mister Citizen can submit additional information to explain or rebut the problems cited. Also, the Notice will inform Mister Citizen where to send his response and most importantly, when the response must be received by Agent America.

Normally, Mister Citizen must submit his response within thirty days from the date of the Notice of Intent to Deny. Usually, by the time Mister Citizen gets the Notice, he only has about 25 days left before the Notice response period expires.

By now, panic has absorbed both Mister Citizen and Miss Foreigner. They normally do not understand how Agent America could deny this petition when everything to them is so obvious! Is s/he blind, or a bigot, or just hateful?

This is usually the time when Miss Foreigner and Mister Citizen desperately contact an immigration attorney. The terms used within the Notice may not make any sense to either Miss Foreigner or Mister Citizen. However, an experienced immigration attorney will understand what Agent America wants to know and why s/he wants to know it.

Immigration attorneys are not miracle workers. In order to properly do their jobs they too need the opportunity to review the Notice, review the previously-submitted evidence, get more evidence if needed, and then prepare the response. They may have to speak with Agent America regarding any part of the Notice that is unclear or confusing. All this takes time!

So, if Miss Foreigner and Mister Citizen want an immigration attorney to help them, they need to meet with the attorney as quickly as possible. Also, our lovebirds may need to work with the attorney to determine what other options are available if Agent America does not change his/her mind.

CHAPTER SEVEN – Questions and Answers

During our careers as immigration attorneys we have been asked many questions about the marriage-based green card. Hopefully, the first six chapters have answered most of your questions.

As with a topic as complex as this one, there are many exceptions to the rules. Also, the rules may have different interpretations under different circumstances.

The following are twelve questions (and answers) most often presented by American citizens and their foreign-born spouses. Hopefully, these may help clarify any remaining issues of the marriage-based green card.

QUESTION #1: How soon after marriage can Mister Citizen petition for Miss Foreigner's immigrant visa?

> **ANSWER:** As soon as the ink is dry on the marriage certificate.

QUESTION #2: My spouse's green card is valid for only two years. Why?

> **ANSWER:** If your marriage is less than two years old when your spouse's green card is issued, then it is considered a "conditional" card. Your spouse and you must file Form I-751 during the 90-day period before the expiration date on your spouse's green card in order to receive a standard 10-year card.

QUESTION #3: I'm an American citizen. Doesn't the American Government have to give my spouse a green card if I demand it?

ANSWER: No. The American Government has established specific criteria that all persons must satisfy before being allowed to enter the United States. If your spouse does not meet the criteria, or cannot obtain a waiver for any specific criteria, then your spouse will not be allowed to immigrate into the United States. Also, your spouse may not be allowed to visit the United States as a tourist, student or any other non-immigrant visitor. NOTE: The American Government will not stop you from leaving the United States to live with your spouse in a foreign land.

QUESTION #4: My American citizen spouse promised to petition for my green card, but she never has. Can I force her to petition for me?

ANSWER: Not according to the immigration regulations. However, there may be other legal means available. Since everyone's situation is different, it is recommended that you get advice from a qualified immigration attorney.

QUESTION #5: I have a green card and just got married to a man from my home country. I was told that he would have to wait almost five years before he would get his immigrant visa. Is this true?

ANSWER: Depends on which is the home country, but the concept is correct. For lawful permanent residents, when your spouse's petition is approved, a "priority date" is assigned to that petition. Each month the American Government announces which priority dates are "current" for the various immigrant categories. Those persons whose priority date is the same or earlier than the announced "current" dates can immediately process for an immigrant visa. For category 2A, the immigrant category for spouses of LPRs, the estimated wait is approximately four years.

QUESTION #6: I am an American citizen. How soon after my spouse gets her green card can she apply for American citizenship?

ANSWER: Three years from the effective date of her green card, as long as you two are still married.

QUESTION #7: I am an American citizen. My future spouse has two children under 18 years old. Can I get them green cards, too?

ANSWER: Yes. Separate petitions must be filed for each child as your step-child.

QUESTION #8: My spouse is abusing me. I want to leave him, but am afraid that he can get me deported. What can I do?

> **ANSWER:** The law is not so brutal that it forces you to stay with a spouse abuser for the sake of a green card. First of all, seek help and counseling at a spouse abuse shelter. Also, contact an immigration attorney.

QUESTION #9: I was told by my first husband (a European) that we were divorced. I have since married an American citizen. Now my first husband tells me he never did file a divorce. What do I do now?

> **ANSWER:** Under American law you can only have one husband at a time. If your first marriage has never been legally terminated, then your marriage to the American citizen will not be accepted by the American Government. Your situation is common, but requires competent legal help to correct. An experienced immigration attorney will need to review your case to determine the best solution to your problem.

QUESTION #10: I have my green card, but my American spouse and I got divorced. He's threatened to tell the government to deport me. Can he do that?

> **ANSWER:** While he may call the government and make all sorts of accusations, your ex-husband does not have the authority or power to get you deported.

QUESTION #11: I have the two-year conditional residence status. My husband and I got divorced before filing to remove the two-year condition. Will I be deported?

ANSWER: The law allows you to file to remove this condition on your own, without your ex-husband signing the petition. As you will need a waiver to submit your petition, it is recommended you get help from a qualified immigration attorney. This petition is serious business and needs to be prepared with care.

QUESTION #12: I think I need legal help, but don't know how to select an attorney. Any suggestions?

ANSWER: The recommendations of friends may provide you with some good choices. Many local bar associations have a lawyer referral service. Also, there are private organizations, churches and groups which provide immigration services for free or a small fee. In addition, the American Immigration Lawyers Association (AILA) has several thousand members throughout the United States and worldwide, and many locales have AILA chapters.

About the Authors

STEPHEN J. ZAWACKI, ESQ. has practiced immigration law as a private attorney mainly in Florida and also as a senior immigration advisor within the U.S. Department of Homeland Security. He is an active member of the District of Columbia Bar and an inactive member of the State Bar of California.

LINDA YIN LIANG, ESQ. is an active member of the State Bar of California and is currently practicing immigration law in Florida. An immigrant herself, she understands how a person feels as a petitioner, applicant and beneficiary of an immigration action.

Attorneys Zawacki and Liang can be reached via the Internet at immigration.doingitright@gmail.com.

Spousal Immigration – Doing It Right

配偶移民 - 要做就做对

Stephen J. Zawacki, 律师

和

Linda Yin Liang, 律师

版权

本书版权归Stephen J. Zawacki 律师和Linda Y. Liang 律师。 任何人不经出版者书面允许不得对本书的任何部分都以任何一种形式或图片、电子或机械，包括复印、录音、录像或其他信息储存系统翻制。

本书的目的是提供咨询而非法律咨询意见。 请向对移民法有经验的律师咨询法律意见。 请注意，移民法本生是多变的法律，本书作者尽力保持信息的准确性。

ISBN-13: 978-1470076160

敬献

感谢那些多年来和我一起交流知识和经验的移民律师们！

前言

本书是基于两个美国移民律师多年的经验写成的。我们荣幸地帮到了无数夫妻在美国团圆。美国移民律师是一个很光荣的职业。

围绕着基于家庭的移民申请一直有很多疑问，传言，怀疑和误解。昨天的法律，今天已经不适用。明天的法律又会变化。這本書的目的是讓讀者對移民過程有更深地理解.

在这本书中，我們常常強調在辦理移民過程中极其需要一位稱職的移民律師.此推荐并非为律師提供商務机會，而是强调这些步骤又多重要。

移民是个法律程序。美国是个法制国家。所以一个称职的律师能在法律程序中影响到一个人的人生是一个符合逻辑和恰当的说法。

TABLE OF CONTENTS

第一章 初探爱情、婚姻和绿卡

我爱他吗？我对他的爱到了可以结婚的程度吗？

他是爱我还是爱我能给他带来的绿卡？

如果她得不到绿卡，又怎样？

美国移民法允许美国公民和永久居民（绿卡持有者）申请其配偶到美国居住并获得永久居住权（绿卡。永久居民能够在美国无限期内居住并工作。

"婚姻绿卡"的历史不是一帆风顺的。在美国移民法的制订过程中，美国政府在制定移民法的时候，考虑到了传染病的可怕，外国人为到美国而利用美国公民的现象和种族歧视等因素。该法律的正式名称是美国移民和归划法。它规定了美国公民或绿卡持有者申请其国外配偶到美国的程序。该程序并不那么简洁明了。该程序常常被比做乡村小道，坑坑包包，十分曲折。

美国公民和永久居民都能为配偶申请移民签证。然而，这两种人在申请过程中受到的待遇有很大的不同。美国公民的配偶可以立即得到签证，而永久居民的配偶要等很长时间才能得到签证。

本书旨在成为一张能说话的指向"婚姻绿卡"的地图。我们一路上有两个向导 - 两个要结婚的人和他们将要遇到的象是交通警察一样的美国政府官员。

我们一心想着移民的人叫外国佛理达小姐和公民切斯特先生。

外国佛理达小姐爱上了一个美国公民。她计划嫁给她的美国男朋友，以其配偶的身份移民到美国。外国小姐从来没有在美国住过。这是她第一次和美国移民系统接触。

公民切斯特先生是一个普通的美国公民，爱上了非美国公民，在国外生活的女士。他计划和他的外国女朋友结婚。这也是他第一次和美国移民系统打交道。

（注：尽管我们的主人翁们是美国男性和非美国女性，现实中也可能是反的。本书举此例是因为大多数情况下是这样。 ）

在大多数官僚机构中，许多事情本来可以由一个政府部门很有效地解决的，但多个政府部门都分管一些职责。有的时候这些职责是重复的，政府部门可能变成对立面。移民系统就是这样的一个官僚机构。

国土安全部的公民和移民服务局负责所有在美国国内提出的移民申请。

国务院领事事务部负责所有在美国大使馆和领事馆提出的移民申请。

美国移民官是我们的政府官员。他（或她，取决于地方）的头衔可能是USCIS检查员或者领事馆或大使馆的官员。他／她的工作任务是面试，审阅申请资料和确定恋人提供的证词是否属实。

我们在接下来的篇幅详细叙述移民过程。

第二章描述美国移民法要求的婚姻。

从第三章到第六章，我们将描述以婚姻为基础的移民过程：恋爱与婚姻，表格的准备，面谈和拒签。

我们在第七章会提到一些和婚姻移民相关的常见问题和答案。

让我们开始吧。

第二章－－一个美国移民婚姻。

适用法律

美国法律允许美国公民为配偶申请进入美国的签证。这些签证随时申请，随时都有。没有时间和数额的限制。

美国法律也允许永久居民为配偶申请签证。但他们的配偶必须要等待一段时间才能拿到签证。 有的会等很多年。

所有的以婚姻为基准的申请能否被批取决于该婚姻是否真实。换句话说，双方是否仅仅为绿卡而结婚的。

政府的决定

美国移民官有个很重要的决定要做。如果外国小姐和公民先生的关系是"真"的，也就是说，双方彼此认识、相处了足够长时间后结的婚，还是他们的婚姻是假的，也就是说，这对恋人想欺骗移民官，让外国小姐到美国来。如果美国移民官认为这个婚姻是真实的， 那么外国人小姐就会很快拿到到美国的签证。

如果美国移民官相信这个婚姻是假的，或者很可能是假的，那么这对恋人就要面对严重的问题。首先，申请过程会拖得长一些，费用也随之高涨(恋人的费用也高一些)。

其次，更重要的是外国小姐可能永远来不了美国，而公民先生可能会因为诈骗而受到法律制裁。

移民官的决定申请人在申请的过程中提交的材料和在面谈的过程中提供的信息决定移民官做出什么样的决定。

真实的或者虚假的婚姻。

一个在新闻报纸所登的广告：寻找伴侣，并愿意支付$5000美金，快速办理。

一个朋友帮助另一个朋友办理只有名义上的婚姻。

一个"安排的婚姻"，双方不住在一起。

多年来，假婚姻很流行。移民官积累了很丰富的经验辨识这样的婚姻。外国小姐和公民先生如果以为他们能轻易蒙混过关，他们大错特错了。

美国移民官经受了很多培训学习如何辨识虚假婚姻，而且她可能有很多年审查婚姻移民申请的经验。当然有时我们的移民官也会被骗，但毕竟是少数。如果该对恋人尝试欺骗美国移民官，他们必须记住欺骗移民官将被罚款$250,000和监禁5年。

移民官是移民方面的专家，而该对恋人却是业余的。当专家和业余选手比赛的时候，谁常常是赢家？答案不言而愈。

在整个申请移民的过程中，恋人们常常需要证明婚姻是诚恳和真实的。移民官没有义务反证该婚姻是为绿卡为目的的。证明婚姻的真实性是恋人们的责任。也就是说，恋人们要提供证据证明他们的婚姻是真实的。

我们通常不会想到要用证据来向他人证明自己的婚姻。但在申请移民的过程中，证据非常重要。移民官可能从来没有见过申请人，移民官的决定全部基于书面资料做出。以下是移民官的一些基本问题：

- 双方在结婚前认识了多长时间？

- 双方的年龄差距有多大？

- 是否是跨文化的婚姻？

- 在结婚前双方相处了多长时间？

- 该婚姻是否是通过中介介绍的？

- 双方结婚了多久？

- 外国配偶以前有没有和美国公民结过婚？

- 外国小姐有没有被驱逐出境过？

在一般情况下，当一个人问一个问题，回答人会给出一个很详细的叙述。但是常常回答问题的人只想提供最简单的回答。在移民申请的过程尤其如此。

当移民官询问外国小姐和她的新配偶的生活隐私的时候，外国小姐常常感到非常愤怒和难为情。公民先生也会因移民官问及太多隐私而很不愉快。

问题不是谁赢谁输。移民官必须要根据事实和经验做判断，而恋人却不想他们的私生活成了公开的记录。

问题到最后归结为如果坚持自己的观点，谁到最后失去得更多？对于移民官来说，这个过程只不过是工作的一部分。移民官不会因为做了一个错误的决定而失去工作或赔钱。移民官只需要向他的上级汇报。标准的情形就是做出一个保守，不会有争议的决定。不管公民先生如何威胁或外国小姐如何恳求，移民官不会把他的脖子伸出来。

在一些国家，让官僚改变主意的办法是给钱给他或她。如果外国人小姐试图"影响"移民官"先生，后果是灾难性的。不仅会被拒签，而且如果在美国贿赂，外国人小姐会被逮捕和关进监狱。

在另一方面，如果美国移民官对回答不满意，外国人小姐和公民先生要付出很大的代价。分居住在不同的地方，要旅行和做其他的事，费用都不小。

法律对美国移民官花多长时间做出决定没有要求。美国移民官可以自由决定他需要多长时间研究每个申请。有可能外国小姐等待几个月甚至几年，最后得到的结论是移民官认为该婚姻是假的。

许多人发现在递交申请之前值得向有经验的移民律师咨询。有的人甚至在结婚前就向移民律师咨询以求防患于未然。

如果婚姻被认为是假的，不能轻视，因为相应的惩罚可能是很严重的，影响很长时间

49

第三章： 恋爱与婚姻

婚姻本应是双方一生相爱、尊重和保护对方的约定。美国政府认为人们结婚前的关系应该有如下的特点：

1) 交往了合理长的一段时间；

2) 双方有适量的沟通。

"合理"这个是词没有特定的定义。不同的申请"合理"的定义不同。因为每个文化和种族都有不同的恋爱概念，某件事情是否合理，需要要经过很多分析才能下定义。

在有些文化环境中，恋爱有很多规矩。爱情要经过很多个月，甚至很多年才能成熟到能结婚的程度。

在另外一些文化环境中，婚姻双方婚前的接触比较随便。在婚前接触的时间相对也很短。如果此婚姻是由家庭亲戚或婚姻中介搭线促成的，双方婚前接触的时间更短。

美国移民官在决定美国公民和外国小姐相处的时间是否足够长的时候，要把这些差异考虑进去。美国移民官需要判断假设外国小姐不需要或不想获得绿卡，他们的关系是否还会持续。

换句话说，如果外国小姐不需要获得绿卡后才能和她的先生住在一起，外国小姐和公民先生是否还是会结婚。

如果他们会，那么外国小姐就会在她的护照上收到闪亮的移民签证。如果他们不会，外国小姐不会得到移民签证。不仅如此，如果移民官认为这对夫妻故意要违反美国移民法，公民先生会被美国政府以故意欺骗提起公诉。

所以，证明一个婚姻最有效的方式是由美国公民和外国伴侣证明他们在结婚前有很扎实的关系。有很多方式可以证明这层关系。最普遍的是：

- 交换的信件和其他沟通方式

- 机票和收据

- 照片

- 证人证言

这些证据不需要是完美的。也没有必要提供恋爱双方每一个激情时分的证据。事实上，如果证据太完美无缺，美国移民官可能还不会相信呢，而且还会对关键的证据的真实性提出质疑。原因是一般的人不会对他们的生活保留太完美的证据。所以，如果你提出的证据看上去象是恋爱小说，那美国移民官会觉得这些都是编的。

请记住，美国移民官是人。他或她需要觉得下结论说该婚姻是真实的是"合适"。他或她想知道恋爱的所有细节。只要在恋爱过程的证据不是太明显地不真实，恋爱双方会得到山姆大叔的允许。

信件或其他方式的沟通。

美国移民官认为恋爱中的人会给对方写信。所以，公民先生和外国小姐彼此之间的书信来往是双方关系的建立和发展的证明。

如今互联网盛行，人们已经不写信了。相应的，他们给对方写电子邮件。所以，电子邮件的复印件也可以作为双方关系的证明。

现在，美国移民官不傻。他或她会查信件的日期。他或她会在面试的时候问关于这些信件的问题。他或她会查双方有没有明显的错误，比如用同样的纸张，同样的墨水或同样的打印机。他或她会查这些电子邮件地址是不是对的。听上去可能很傻，有的人上交的信，本来是恋爱傻写给对方的，结果他们看上去的时候是一个人手迹。

如果信只有一方写的，那美国移民官就很可能怀疑这层关系的真实性。如果提供的信包含了双方写的信，这些证据的可信度就高很多。如果可能的话，提供有回邮地址，邮资的信封，这样，证据要充分很多。

所以，外国小姐和公民先生需要把他们之间交换的信件和卡片存好。這些信件不單有私人診藏价值而且可能这些证据足以証明他们的婚姻经过了合理的恋爱过程。

票据和收据

交换的信件很好，但如果外国小姐和公民先生能証明他们在何时和何地在一起，就更好。

美国移民官很难相信两个人在不见面的情况下能建立很深的关系，并且爱得深到愿意结婚的程度。美国移民官会查恋爱双方是否在结婚前至少见了一面。

假设外国小姐和公民先生在法国认识。他们后来在伦敦的一个摇滚乐音乐会上又见到了。他们后来又一起到Candun和Tihiti玩。在这些共同旅行后，他们一定又很多酒店的收据啊、登机牌啊、护照上的章啊等等可以証明他们在一起旅行过。

如果外国小姐和公民先生能证明他们在某些地方一起呆过，他们的关系就更可信。事实上，没有这样的证据，美国移民官很可能不会给外国小姐移民签证。移民官一定会明确地询问外国小姐有没有和公民先生一起去过什么地方。

如果有些票据和收据没有保存下来，有些办法可以弥补。以下是几个例子：

- 如果信用卡付的账，信用卡的账单可以用来代替收据；

- 如果机票丢了，机票又是通过机票中介买的，机票中介的记录也可以証明；

- 公司内部的度假记录可以用来証他们在同一时间度了假。

- 支票，尤其是在备忘栏上有另外一个人的名字，可以用来解释相应的费用。

- 如果护照上有进入另一个国家的印章，也可以用来証在该国逗留过。

所以，永远都不要轻视保持记录的重要性。

照片

有人说，言语固然好，但照片能顶得上千言万语。外国小姐和公民先生在一起做事的照片提供很强的证据证明他们有足够的恋爱经历。最好地照片是那些旅游的照片。

如果外国小姐有她和公民先生照的照片，她应该把它们带去面谈。美国移民官会看这些照片有没有被编辑过，在照片上有没有时间标记。

外国小姐应该核对一下照片正面或反面的日期，确保她的成述和照片提供的信息是一致的。她也要保证她的证词里的日期和照片上的日期是一致的。

证人证言

证词是经由公证人公证过的证人的成述。公证人证明证人本人签的名。

如果证人证言和外国小姐说的相符，证人证言能起到很大的作用。如果一个证人能证明她或他看到外国小姐和公民先生在爱佛尔铁塔上他们的证词可以作为恋爱双方成述的补充。

证人证言的格式和内容很重要。证人证言首先要澄清做此证言的证人是谁。证言自身要简洁明了，不能有奇意。最后，证人要在公证人面前签字。如果对如何提供证言证词有疑问，咨询律师。

婚姻

一般情况下人们认为只有公民先生和外国小姐合法结婚后，公民先生才能为外国小姐申请移民。但每天都有非法结婚的夫妻申请移民资格。

美国移民官要看公民先生和外国小姐的婚姻是不是合法的。而且美国移民官还要看公民先生和公民小姐的前面的婚姻是否已合法终止了。

之前的婚姻是否合法地结束了常常是公民先生能否有资格提出移民申请的问题。每个国家的离婚法不同，即便在美国，不同洲的离婚法都不一样。

有的离婚在一个地方是合法的，在另一个地方就不是。比方说，假如外国小姐一直是單身女性，但公民先生却是在加尼福尼亚洲和另一位女士有婚姻关系。但这位女士却离开了公民先生，在多明尼哥通过代理和公民先生离了婚。公民先生和外国小姐然后在厄瓜多尔接了婚。

根据美国移民法，外国小姐和公民先生在一时间内只能和一个人结婚。比如说，美国移民官会质疑公民先生和他的第一夫人实际还有婚姻关系，因为美国政府不认可代理离婚，所以加洲的婚姻证书还有效。

接下来的问题是厄瓜多尔是否承认公民先生的离婚。如果美国移民官有任何疑问，那么他或她有可能会说 1）公民先生的前婚姻还有效； 2）公民先生和外国小姐的婚姻是重婚； 3）外国小姐不能被授予以婚姻移民签证。

这样，外国小姐和公民先生的申请有了问题，相应地，外国小姐和公民先生的签证申请会推迟，费用也会很高。

许多象外国小姐一样的女士也许因为公民先生们没有完成的离婚的状况而永久都得不到签证，

婚姻中介

在许多文化环境中，许多人通过中介为家庭成员选择结婚对象。这种办法保护家庭成员找到坏人。 换句话说，防止那些傍大款的人。

美国移民官会考量通过中介的婚姻是当地习俗还是为了绿卡而做的交易。

公民先生有可能回应了一个这么说的广告："美丽的亚洲女孩寻找美国先生。请电：1800 - 555 - 5555"，之后，给自己买了个新娘。

外国小姐也许通过报纸如下的广告："你想要绿卡吗？美国先生需要你。"找到了自己的丈夫。"

如果公民先生聘用了一个婚姻中介公司替他在国外找一个的太太，美国移民官会很仔细地调查本申请。以赚钱为目的婚姻是违反移民法的。如果一个婚姻是通过广告促成的，移民官认可该婚姻的可能性很小。

由婚姻中介促成的婚姻还可能造成另一个问题：家庭暴力。当两个不认识的人住在一起，双方都不知道对方会如何待人处事。在那些漂亮的求婚文字下，在婚礼上绅士下面隐藏的可能是一个魔鬼。外国小姐（现在是公民夫人）可能发现她嫁给了一个打老婆的魔鬼，甚至更糟。

因此，这种确定婚姻是否真实的方式可能是有点老套了点，但那些刑庭和医院出具的记录也说明很多问题。

总结

美国移民法将恋爱和婚姻中的浪漫因素提出来放进了一个类似计算机软件系统一样的体系中。也许完全理解该体系是不可能的，但意识到该体系的存在对成功地申请有很大的帮助。

如果外国小姐和公民先生对他们的婚姻是否会能得到移民官的认可有疑问，请向移民律师咨询。

第四章－－填表

外国小姐申请移民需要填表。 每张表需要在不同的阶段填写。

美国政府有时会改动表格的要求。美国政府常常改动表格本身。有的大使馆或领事馆可能因其所在国家的原因有独特的要求。外国小姐应该向当地的大使馆或领事馆了解他们特别的程序要求。

所有的表格都可以在美国移民局的网站－－www.uscis.gov上找到并下载。在此网站上也能找到移民信息。该网站不提供具体咨询，但许多常见问题的答案都可以在上面找到。

以下介绍以婚姻为基础的移民申请的常用表格。要记住每张表都有一定的费用。 只有交了这些费用后，这些申请才能被处理。

为外国的亲戚提出的申请

为外国亲戚提出的申请是整个过程的开始。

目前，提出申请的申请表是I-130.公民先生向美国移民局提出申请。

该申请表收集公民先生和外国小姐的基本信息。该表要求申请人提供是美国公民的证据。

该表也要求申请人提供外国小姐和公民先生的婚姻的信息。以下的文件应该随I130提交，当然提交的文件不限于此：1）USCIS要求的特别尺寸的护照照片；2）一张经过公证的结婚证书；3）离婚证书；4）双方的出生证明。

所有非英语的文件要翻译而且该翻译要经过公证。

财务保证证明

也许这听起来很不浪漫，但公民先生必须证明他必须能养得起太太，否则外国小姐将得不到绿卡。美国法律要求公民先生证明他赚足够的钱能养得起他的太太及继子女。

财务保证书是很严肃的文件。它实际上是公民先生和美国政府之间签订的合同。这份合同规定美国政府不能为外国小姐提供福利服务。如果外国小姐接受了美国政府的帮助，美国政府有权利向公民先生追收该费用。

财务证明的效力持续到以下四个情况之一：1）外国小姐成为美国公民；2）外国小姐已在美国工作了10年并交了社会保险金；3）外国小姐失去永久居住权；（比如：她被驱逐出境或她放弃了美国永久居住权；）4）外国小姐离世。

如果公民先生和外国小姐在外国小姐拿到绿卡后离了婚，财务支持证明照样有效。

到底公民先生需要赚多少钱的标准每年都在变。每年4月，美国政府要公布当年的标准。这个标准在美国大使馆／领事馆，移民局办公室和移民局的网站上都可以找得到。

如果公民先生赚钱不够，那么他可以1）找到另一个美国公民或绿卡持有者代替他提供补充财务证明；或者2）向外国小姐解释因为他太穷，外国小姐不能获得绿卡。

申请签证

一般情况下，以婚姻为原因的移民申请中，外国小姐在美国之外。外国小姐必须要在美国大使馆／领事馆办理签证。这个步骤叫做"领事步骤"。领事程序必须遵照大使馆／领事馆公布的规定进行。

调整身份

有时候，外国小姐在和公民先生结婚的时候合法或非法地住在美国。如果是这样，外国小姐就要在移民局办公室，而不是要回国，办理移民签证的步骤，这叫做"调整身份"。

目前，只有合法进入美国的非公民才能调整身份。（有一两个例外的情况。）合法进入美国指非公民到达美国正式的海关入口，由美国海关安检检查过，海关安检员同意该非公民入了境。

曾经有段时间非法入境的非公民也能调整身份。但此规定在1998年一月14日终止了。有人在动议该规定重新生效。如果外国小姐是非法入境的，她应该寻求移民律师的帮助。

外国小姐和公民先生必须要确定在大使馆／领事馆申领签证或在美国国内调整身份哪个更经济方便。这两种方式各有利弊。申请人最好向一个好的律师咨询后做决定。

体检

外国小姐需要在美国移民局指定的医生处体检。不是所有的医生都能做移民体检，所以，外国小姐要在移民局的网站上找到移民局认可的医生做体检。

部分体检的目的是証明外国小姐打了哪些免疫针。美国疾病管理中心发布了外国小姐的出生国的免疫针的名单。该名单在移民局的办公室及其网站上都可以找到。

当医生做完体检后，会把体检表封在一个信封里，交给外国小姐。如果信封被打开，美国移民官将拒绝接受该体检表。如果这种情况发生，外国小姐必须重新找一个医生再做体检。

如果美国移民官相信该体检报告被改动过，他／她可能直接与医生联系，获得另一个体检报告的拷贝。如果証明体检报告被改动过，美国移民官会对公民先生以欺诈提起公诉，而且因此拒绝外国小姐的移民签证的申请。

代理

如果外国小姐或公民先生希望律师代表他们处理移民签证的申请事务,那么相应一张表格要交上去。目前，这张表格的代号是G-28. G-28要指明申请的种类是什么，谁是代理人，谁是被代理人，被代理人是申请人还是收益人），律师的名字，律师工作的律师行及代理范围。

美国政府不见到该表格，就不会与该律师沟通本申请的有关事务。不仅如此，美国政府也不会接受律师递交的任何文件。

总结

申请移民签证所需要上交的文件很多。文件的审理也很耗时。也就是说，不会很快有结果而且所有的细节都会被仔细地审查。

美国移民官经常收到没有填写完整的表格。他们会拒绝接受这样的表格。虽然美国移民官接受本人准备的申请，聘请一个好的移民律师可能会让整个申请经济实惠而且快一些。

第五章：婚姻面试

在一般情况下，人们不会想到要留下他们确定关系后交往的证据。对大多数人来说，我们尽享欢乐时光，不会想到交往的细节会被某些官僚细查。就是这样一个想法就足以让人倒胃口。

外国小姐和公民先生开始申请绿卡后，他们可能会收到美国政府要求他们面谈的通知。

这种面谈的目的是测试婚姻的真实性。它要确认该婚姻是符合移民法的规定。面试有多种方式。美国移民官有可能同时询问外国小姐和公民先生，也可能分开问。他们也可能录下该夫妻的回答。

婚姻移民的面试可能是很让人紧张的，尤其是当婚姻完全是真实的。极少人喜欢在陌生人面前谈他们的私生活，尤其在一个能决定他们的将来的陌生人面前。

美国移民官会问在表上已经问过的问题。另外，她／他也可能问其他关于该婚姻真实性的证据的问题：

- 这些照片是谁照的？

- 你为什么要到这个地方？

- 你们住同一房间还是分开住的？

- 你们坐哪家航空公司的飞机？

换句话说，这些问题都是和你提供的证据有关。只有确确实实一起做了这些事的人才会知道答案。

有的问题也会涉及到关系的隐私部分：

- 你睡床的哪一面？

- 你们昨天晚上吃的什么？

- 她身上有没有纹身？

- 他打鼾吗？

- 她最不喜欢的亲戚是谁？

- 上次你太太给你买礼物是什么时候，
  买的是什么？

- 你岳母叫什么？

- 你先生最喜欢看什么电视节目？

要正确回答这些问题，一个人要对另一个人非常了解。如果外国小姐和公民先生事实上不住在一起，他们回答对的可能性很小。

外国小姐和公民先生有法律义务向美国移民官提供足以说服他该婚姻是真实的证据和证词。美国移民官没有责任做出反证。

外国小姐和公民先生要有足够的证人证词証明他们的婚姻是真实的。

在美国，如果两个人以夫妻名义住在一起，他们应该有住在一个屋檐下的证明。如果双方拿不出这些证据，美国移民官就会怀疑这对夫妻是否真的接了婚的。以下是一些证据的例子：

- 婚后双方的合照；

- 有双方签字的租赁合同；

- 银行存款証明；

- 取消的支票（有的支票有两个人的签字）

- 驾驶执照（显示两个人的地址都是一样的）

- 保险文件（显示两个人的名字）

主持面谈和审查申请的美国移民官们懂得所有的窍门。他们听了很多故事，也看过各种各样的证据。如果外国小姐和公民先生在证据上做了假，很难说，美国移民官发现不了。这样，外国小姐再也得不到签证，而且美国政府会对这对夫妻以诈骗未遂为名提起公诉。

美国移民官可以对整个面谈过程录像。在很多移民局的办公室，录像是标准程序。录像可以保存证据。外国小姐和公民先生在面谈过程中说的一切可以用来作为拒签的依据。这个录像也可以用来作为驱逐出境的证据。

外国小姐和公民先生需要象准备工作面试一样准备移民面谈。夫妻需要重新看他们交给美国移民官的证据。他们需要很自如地回答书面回答的问题。如果他们要带额外的恋爱和婚姻证据，夫妻需要很认真细致地重新审视这些证据。双方都需要回答"什么时候，在哪儿，谁和为什么"。

总结

.

婚姻面谈就像是剧院演戏。所有的人都准备好而且自如，才能达到最好的结果。

永远记住，美国移民官不认识外国小姐和公民先生。美国移民官第一次见这对夫妇。他／她对他们的认识全来源于他们所提交的表格。

如果外国小姐和公民先生好好地准备，面谈就不会那么困难。如果有任何疑问和担心，他们应该寻求一个有经验的律师的帮助。

第六章： 拒签

如果说在整个过程有让人担惊受怕的一天，这一天就是公民先生收到移民局标题为"关于拒签意向的通知"
.
这个文件没有表格编号。这个文件就是一封题为"关于拒签的意向的通知"。该通知的目的是让申请人知道移民局有意向拒绝给外国小姐发签证。

意向这个词很重要。它说明美国移民官还没有拒绝该申请。该通知说明的是在申请，提供的证据和在面谈过程的叙述中有问题。这些问题严重到移民官对他们的婚姻的真实性提供了质疑。

移民官现在给公民先生一次机会对信中提出的指控做出回复。这封信详细地叙述在申请的问题和适用法律。

该通知也告知公民先生可以提供信息解释或反驳该指控。该通知知会公民先生他应该把他的回复发到什么地方，更重要的是，在什么日期前发到移民官手上。

一般来说，公民先生必须在30天内提交回复。常常在公民先生收到通知的时候，他只有25天做出回复"

现在，公民先生和外国小姐一定慌了。他们通常不会理解美国移民官为什么要拒签，尽管原因写得很清楚了。"他们是瞎了，还是独断专行或者就是心中充满了恨"

通常在这个时候，外国小姐和美国先生在绝望中联系移民律师。公民先生和外国小姐或者都不明白通知中用的术语。有经验的移民律师能够明白移民官先生要知道而且为什么要。

移民律师也不能创造奇迹。为了要解决问题，他们需要看通知和以前上交的证据，并准備回复,他們可能要与移民官通話弄清信中的疑點和問題.這需要時間辦理。

所以说，如果外国小姐和公民先生希望一个移民律师帮助他们，他们需要尽快地和这位律师接触。另外，我们的恋人们也需要和律师一起确定如果美国移民官不改变他的想法，他们能做些什么。

第七章 - - - 问题与答案

我们移民律师常常被问到关于婚姻绿卡的问题。我们希望前面的六章已经回答了大部分问题。

象婚姻绿卡这样复杂的话题，和其他复杂的话题一样，每一个规定都有例外。就是同样的规定，在不同的情形下，解释也不同。

以下是美国先生和他们的外国出生的配偶最常见的12个问题和答案。我们希望读完后他们能帮助理解通过婚姻的绿卡的问题。

问题1：结婚多久后公民先生可以为外国小姐申请移民签证？

> 答案：只要结婚证上的墨水干了就可以了。

问题2：我的配偶的绿卡为什么有效期只有两年？

> 答案：如果你和你的配偶结婚不到两年，你的配偶的绿卡就是有条件的。如果你和你的配偶在两年绿卡到期前3个月申请I-751表，你的配偶的绿卡可以会变成永久性绿卡。

问题3：我是美国公民。是不是只要我要求，美国政府必须给我的配偶办绿卡？

> 答案：不是。每个到美国的人必须要满足美国政府制定的严格的条件。如果你的配偶不能满足这些条件，或者不能得到豁免，你的配偶就不能移民到美国。另外，你的配偶不可以以旅游者、学生或其他非移民的访问者的身份到美国访问。注意：美国政府不会阻拦你到外国和你的配偶一起生活。

问题4：我的美国公民配偶承诺我帮我申请绿卡，但她一直都没有。我可以逼她为我申请吗？

> 答案：根据美国的法律，不行。但也有可能有一些合法的手段。每个人的情形不同，建议你找一个好的移民律师咨询。

问题5：我是绿卡持有者。我刚刚和一个从我的母国来的人接了婚。我听说他要等差不多5年才能办到移民绿卡。是这样吗？

回答：看你的母国是哪个国家了，但大致是这样的。当绿卡持有者为配偶递交的申请批准后，这个申请有了一个签证期。每个月美国政府公布他们处理到哪些签证，那些签证期比公布的日期要早的人可以开始办理签证。对2A类签证，绿卡持有者的配偶的签证的等待时间一般是4年。

问题6：我是美国公民。我的配偶获得绿卡后多久能申请公民？

答案：拿到绿卡后三年，只要你们的当时还没有离婚。

问题7：我是一个美国公民。我的未婚夫有两个不满18岁的小孩。我能帮他们申请到绿卡吗？

可以的。但你要为他们单独申请。

问题8：我的配偶虐待我。我想离开他但我担心他会让我被驱逐出境。我该怎么办？

答案：法律没有残忍到逼你和一个虐待你的配偶在一起才会给你绿卡。首先，你应该找到一个配偶虐待帮助中心，接着你应该和一位移民律师联系。

问题9：我的第一个丈夫告诉我要我和他离婚了。我于是和一个美国公民结了婚。现在我的第一个丈夫告诉我他从来没有告诉过离婚。我现在该怎么办？

答案：美国法律规定你只能在一时间内有一个丈夫。如果你原来的婚姻从来没有结束过，你和美国公民的婚姻不会被美国政府承认。你这种情况很常见。但你需要法律支持帮助你解决这个问题。你需要请一个有经验的移民律师审视你的状况，帮忙找到最佳的解决方案。

问题10：我已经获得了绿卡，但我和美国配偶离婚了。他威胁我要让政府驱逐我出境。他可以这么做吗？

回答：你的前夫可能会打电话给政府投诉你，但你的前夫没有权利驱逐你出境。

问题11：我有两年的临时绿卡。我先生和我在申请取消两年绿卡限制之前离了婚，我会不会被驱逐出境？

回答：根据法律规定，你可以在没有你先生支持的情况下申请取消两年绿卡限制。因为你需要一个做免责申请，你最好请一个好的律师代理。这样的申请很不容易，一定要小心。

问题12：我想要寻求法律协助，但不知道如何选择好的律师。你有什么建议吗？

回答：你的朋友的推荐可能给你提供一些选择。许多律师协会会为你提供推荐服务。许多协会，教会和团队会提供一些免费或低价的服务。另外，美国移民律师协会也在各州有自己的分会。

作者简介

STEPHEN J. ZAWACKI, ESQ. 律师一直在佛罗里达州做移民业务。他同时还是美国国土安全局的高级顾问。他在哥伦比亚特区的律师协会的注册律师，曾是加尼佛尼雅州的律师协会的成员。

LINDA YIN LIANG, ESQ. 律师是基尼佛尼雅州的律师协会的注册律师，现在佛罗里达州提供移民事务服务。她本人也是移民，所以他能理解移民过程中当事人的感受。

Zawacki 律师和梁律师的 email 地址是：
immigration.doingitright@gmail.com.

www.ingramcontent.com/pod-product-compliance
Lightning Source LLC
Chambersburg PA
CBHW071625170526
45166CB00003B/1190